Easy Coloring Book
for Beginners

This Coloring book belongs to:_____

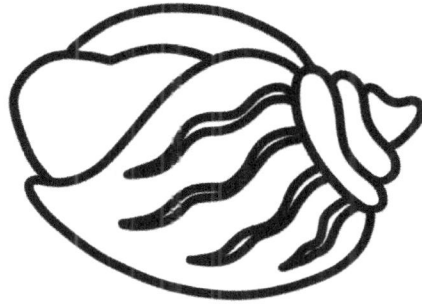

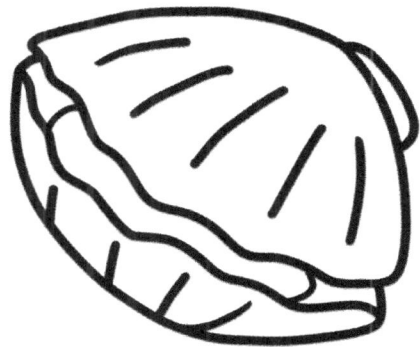

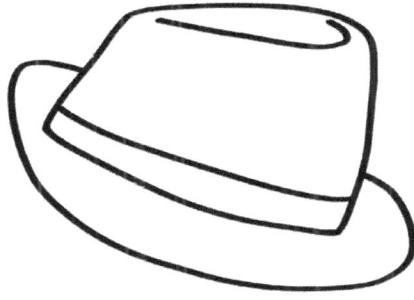

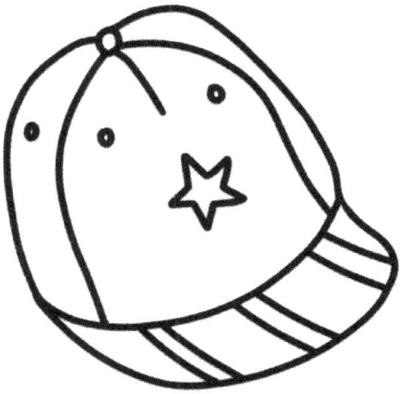

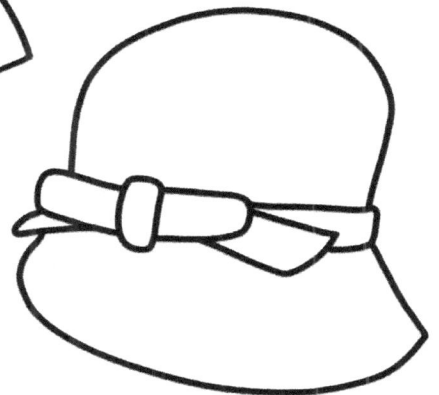

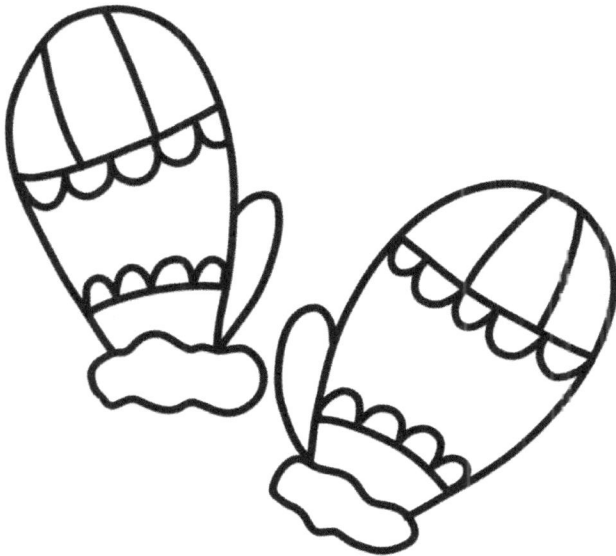

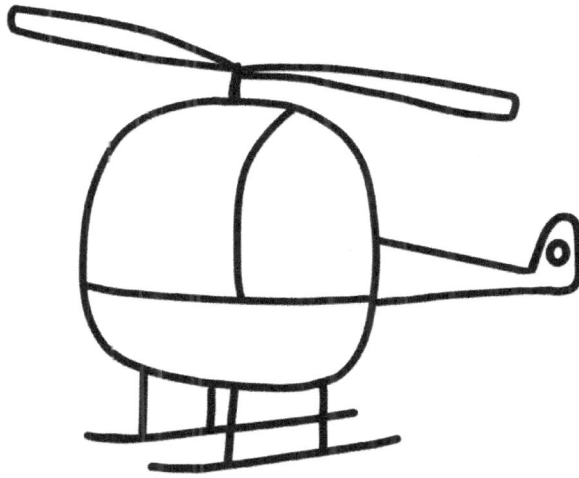

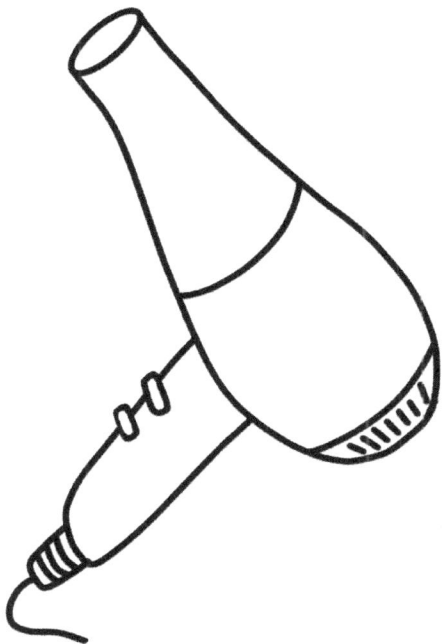

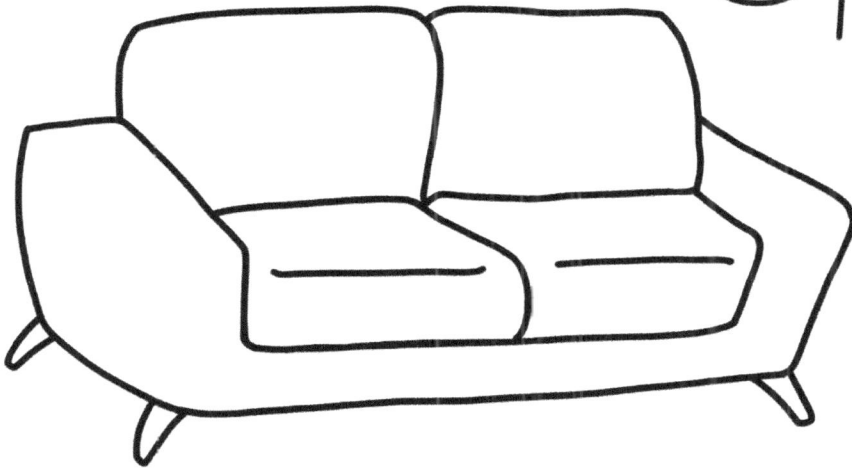

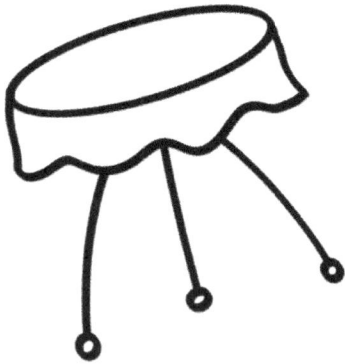

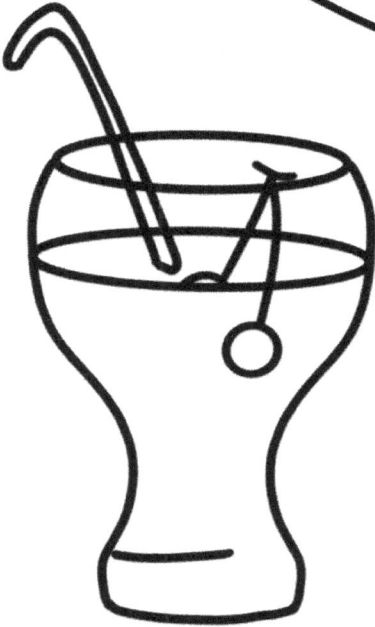

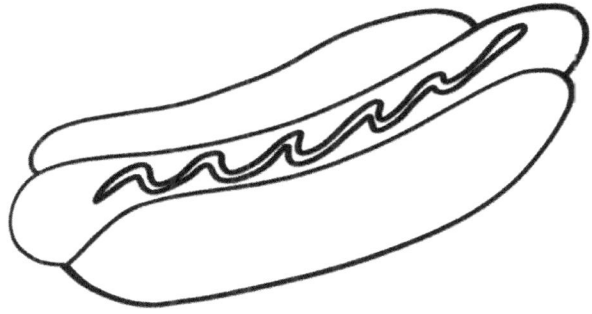

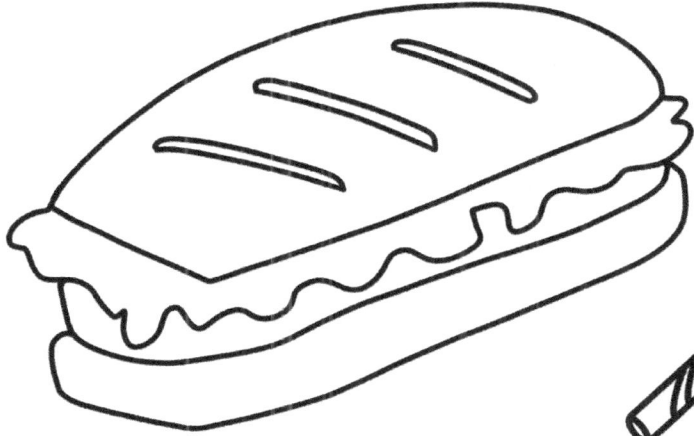

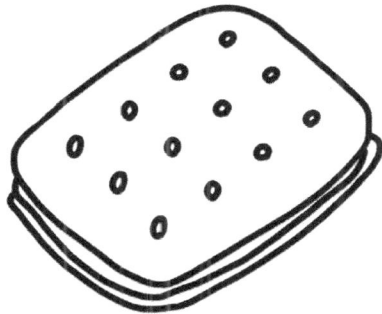

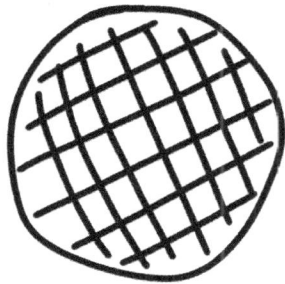

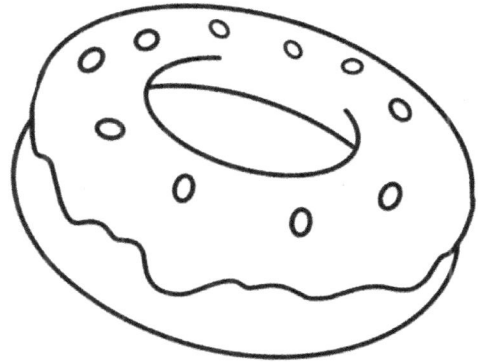

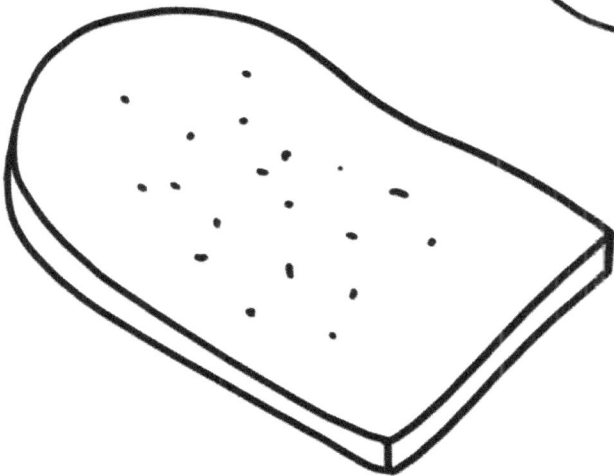

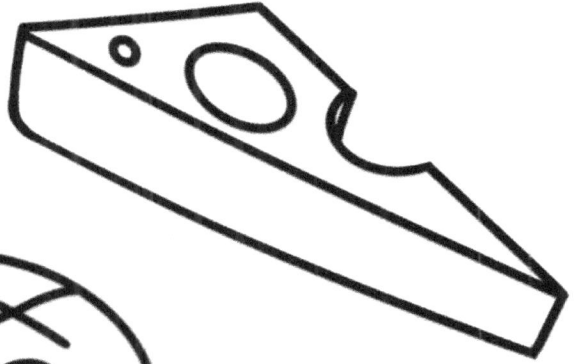

Thank you!

Finally, if you enjoyed this easy coloring book, then I'd like to ask you for a favor, would you be kind enough to leave a review for this book on Amazon? It'd be much appreciated!

Feel free to check my other books on my Amazon page https://www.amazon.com/author/jay.t

Thanks again and Wish you and family Living a Colorful and Wonderful Life

Made in the USA
Las Vegas, NV
10 July 2021

26226206R00037